Eyes Speak Honey

a trail of poems,
soft storms
and strange truths

Dana Qadah

ISBN: 978-1964354446

Library of Congress Catalog Card Number:
2025922295

DEDICATION

For anyone who's ever felt like too much and not enough at the same time.

map of the heart

a trail of poems, soft storms, and strange truths

---

things that know me

where it all begins: knots, clouds, nostalgia

x - suncatcher
o - crabapple tree
x - belonging
o - wrinkles
x - la luna
o - little one
x - hope is still alive even if it aches sometimes
o - the moths
x - sunday kind of love
o - for will

---

some kind of crystal ball

where it shatters: reflection, grime, ache

x - born in the right era
o - gold nothing
x - romanticizing being legally blind

o - senti-mental
x - bathroom floor
o - pyromaniac
x - bulldozer with a smile
o - i ♡ therapy
x - as above, so below
o – tornada
x - the only way is through

---

infinite, anyway

where it becomes something new: echoes, dreams, mementos

x - grey hair
o - legacy
x - hanahaki
o - stability
x - ritual
o - acceptance
x - her
o - home
x - infinite, anyway

PART I

Things That Know Me

I've always looked for shapes in clouds and faces in knots of wood. I love the way the world seems to respond when I speak gently to it. These are the things that watched me grow, even when I didn't know I was becoming anything at all.

SUNCATCHER

Absorbing other's light and

Refracting it back in sparks of jewels

Crowning the cat's dozy head

As he dreams of all the kibble

He's batted under the fridge

CRABAPPLE TREE

Luscious lilacs line the lane

Boasting their fragrance noisily

Intentionally placed,

Unmistakably calculated

The clear choice and favorite

Among them, a disturbance

A glint of pink among the purples

My crabapple tree

That was never supposed to exist

Its fruit tastes like shit

It messes up the flow

It's unruly, untamed and

It never fails to catch my eye.

BELONGING

Feel the grass intertwined between your toes,

The rays of sun mingle with your eyelashes,

The breeze entrapping you in his arms.

We so often forget

We do not own this world,

The world owns us.

WRINKLES

The history of your deepest laughter

Etched into your face

There is no shame in being worn by the world.

When slow streams carve out mighty rocks

We marvel at the power

Life is a gift, a gift, a gift.

LA LUNA

Alguna

Me conoce como la luna.

Consigo

Lejos, un mejor amigo.

Noche

Salgo sin reproches.

Luna

Ilumina las calles, cada una.

Nota

Cuando me siento tan rota.

Razón

Contenido en mi corazón.

Luna

Amiga desde mi cuna.

LITTLE ONE

So full of affection

My silent guardian

Rumbling warmth

From rose nose

To stub tail

I'll always love you

Little one

HOPE IS STILL ALIVE EVEN IF IT ACHES SOMETIMES

When I was

Young

and

Bright

and

Finding the light was my default…

Magic filled every inch of my days.

I lost it somewhere.

But sitting here in my first home,

The windows frame the blue backdrop of dusk so beautifully,

The cricket song ebbs and flows.

I see a young buck proudly standing,

Staring back at me among twinkling fireflies.

There's just enough light to see the velvety golden sheen of his early-summer antlers.

The trees watch from behind him too,

And shimmer their green leaves to say good night.

Hope is still alive even if it aches sometimes.

MOTHS

The moths always bump into the window at night.

They sound like fingers tapping on the glass.

All they want is a bit of the glowing light

Like every one of us, but alas

We think them stupid, meek, and dull...

Their writhing bodies keep trying, dying.

So determined to reach the incandescent null – the Beautiful -

Give us wings, and we'd look just like the flying;

Dying, trying.

SUNDAY KIND OF LOVE

There's something about a Sunday

The way my coffee mixes just right

The smiling sun and the cozy feel

On the edge of a life without bounds

Savor each drop.

FOR WILL

When I think of you, it's the golden hour
Willow leaves shine and wave
Shadows move in fields of flowers
Now I can only visit your grave.

With our fingers outstretched on a cool trampoline,
We'd laugh and ponder along with the stars.
Hours of bright video game characters flashed on a screen
We always knew the summer was ours.

I'm so sorry that in your darkest hour
All the golden ones faded away.
I'm so sorry that time devoured,
All the golden things decayed.

PART II

Some Kind of Crystal Ball

The magic here isn't clean or easy. It's reflective, gritty, and alchemical. No matter how many times I fall, I choose to be a lover in a fighter's world.

BORN IN THE RIGHT ERA

My body is a temple

But just like...

Filled with Diet Coke

and Cheetos

and just a little bit of weed.

GOLD NOTHING

I mistyped "Good morning" and it autocorrected
to *gold nothing.*

A bird smacked into the window
just trying to get
where he was going next.

I'm wired but I'm tired and I'm going nowhere fast

and my boss says
I messed up again,

So now my nervous system
thinks there's a predator
on my ass.

ROMANTICIZING BEING LEGALLY BLIND

Glasses set to the side

In a cup holder in my car

Rain dots the windshield

All is watercolor

A dull yellow porch light

Creates a scintillating mosaic

This breath of a moment

Painted with us in mind

SENTI-MENTAL

x - Extra toothbrushes in case a guest wants to stay the night unexpectedly

o - Miles of mental lists of dietary preferences and favorite foods

x - Saying "I love you" at the end of every call

o - Writing down each and every song, book, show, movie recommendation and following through with them

x - Exclaiming "look at the sky!" at least once a day in absolute awe

o - Being the version of myself that younger me would've looked up to. ♡

BULLDOZER WITH A SMILE

Grinning while I wreck it all,
Face painted with what I've carried
Things will go my way.

Cement cracks around soft interior,
Bulldoze. Control. My eyes get blearier.

I won't mother you through this.

"If you're gonna be stupid
 you gotta be tough."

So I scream like a teapot boiling over;
A million voices spit fire through one mouth.

Because
I said so, that's why.

I don't have to explain what's truth versus lie.

BATHROOM FLOOR

Bathroom floor, bathroom floor.

You're cold and peripheral

and kind of smell like pee

But I'm pretty sure you've been

the only thing that caught me

When my body didn't want to hold my soul anymore.

Bathroom floor, bathroom floor.

PYROMANIAC

Enjoying the glow

Is completely separate from

Throwing myself in the flames.

I know this but yet

I crave it in my blood

And it flashes a smile

I grow to love the way it moves.

So I embrace it

Let it consume me

Till there's ash and soot and bone

And a memory of what once was

I ♡ THERAPY

bend

until

you

bend

until

you

bend

until

you

bend

until

you

bend

until

you…

b r e a k

Now the kitchen is a fucking mess

Trauma shattered tiles

Step on it

Till your nerve endings are

Severed,

Mangling,

Numb.

AS ABOVE, SO BELOW

Shoveling dirt into my mouth
I thought I buried you
I know I buried you

Smeared filth on my lips
Scrub them raw for being
Forced open by you

Submerge myself in the bath
Fully clothed, wholly shaken
Let every bubble of breath out

I'm so much safer drowning.

TORNADA

A cloudy presence approaches

Its humid reputation encroaches

Grumbling impatiently upon arrival

Hide! Flee! Hide! Get down for survival!

Everyone takes cover beneath

While above, it flashes spinning teeth

Winds howl and tearfully sing

Messy, sporadic, tornado of a thing

Stretching toward heaven and spiraling downward

Then… suddenly rests, a silence encountered

Weeps quietly and looms for the night

Rhythmic and flowing and cozy and light

An intrusive neighbor that's hard to keep

But I promise, I'll still always lull you to sleep.

THE ONLY WAY IS THROUGH

How bad was the storm?

You ok?

It tore everything down. There's nothing left of what once was. I don't know how to cope.

But… I'm alive. That can be enough for right now.

I love you through it all.

Me too.

Promise?

Promise.

PART III

Infinite, Anyway

Nothing lasts. And nevertheless, everything stays. This is the part where I live in the aftermath and learn to call it home. There's no neat ending, only a kind of beautiful continuation.

GREY HAIR

Goddess gargoyle

Gorgeous silver coil

Nested atop my swirly brain head

I thought for sure I would be long dead

before you ever shone your beauty

Now, you give me a sense of duty

To live!

I LIVED!

I lived.

LEGACY

Inverted gaze

Mocking mannerisms

Weak knees,

Perceptive eyes.

Soft tones,

Sharp wit.

Shrug into her sweater

Brush her curls out of my eyes

Sweet tooth, sweeter tongue

Carry the legacy high.

HANAHAKI

Coughing up petals and leaves

Occasionally, whole blossom heaves

Twisting and writhing, gripping sharp vines

Invading my lungs to clutch intestines

They thought it was a gift

To plant a garden in my midriff

Their well-intentioned words

Echo back like flourishes of slurs.

While they dance at the thought of my miracle,

I taste the sickly sweet rot stuck in my spiracle.

One particular day, I've had enough.

Clawing out twigs, nails catching pollen tuft

Unwrap the corkscrew that cages my guts

Get everything out no matter how it cuts

Drenched red hands, if there's a God, let me rest

Slithering tendrils of green persevere nonetheless

Shattering my teeth and splitting my lips

Finally, the roots end and hang to my hips.

"I'm done," I declare into a dreamy haze

Till I'm choked by new blooms reaching out for the sun's rays.

STABILITY

You are a sturdy shoulder when I'm on the floor,

An illuminated home in the midst of a downpour.

You are the familiar face in a swelling crowd,

My light at the end of the tunnel, shining loud.

RITUAL

Audible crack as they split in half

Boiling liquid viciously attacks

Withered green into crushed sanguine

Flames to rounded cattle, finish routine

Easing into an ancient settee

You have just made… spaghetti.

ACCEPTANCE

Red wine presence

With white wine wishes

Deep berry stains shout underneath

Words drip molasses - dense & sweet

Dark lunar evening

With sunrise ambitions

Loud blue laughter breaks the silence

Eyes speak honey - honest & warm

HER

What is and what once was

Hold each other in delicate balance

Luminescence from above gives way to

Horoscoping freckles on her nose

HOME

Nose wrinkles, high pitch-

"Eww-uh! Why is this spot so warm?!"

Long-eyelashed blue, hint of lisp-

"I heard that if you pee in the pond,"

Big inhale,

"It'll turn RED all around you!"

Slicked ponytail, closed-lip grin-

"Aboard our ship! Next island!"

Flop onto our vessel

Fling life jackets

They drip splotches on the wood

Curls stink of fish and earth

Big sister packed fruit snacks and navigates

Little brother is the kicking motor and provides energy

Middle sister creates waves, shifting her weight from leg to leg.

The sunshine from our eyes dries my suit.

INFINITE, ANYWAY

The shore rings with the smell of rain. Unfamiliar faces pass by - shades of white and gray - shades not to be recognized or acknowledged. A kaleidoscope of expressions lie here, each face a drop.

Some smile, but some look out onto the water, as if it will answer a question they have asked far and wide.

And in this quiet moment of reflection into the deep waves, his face mirrors the color of my own. The curves, the freckles, the imperfections no one but him and I would notice. He uses a cane to sift along, careful not to disturb anyone or anything with his presence.

The footprints are the first to go. The sand will not hold his form very long.

His youth is next to be dismissed. Gone are the rosebud cheeks and lips paired with the infectious smile. Time flies by him like a hummingbird, unaware of anything but its own frantic wings and ways.

And what is next to leave?

Our memory. The waves engulf the secret gestures, the bright, reminiscent eyes, the tender moments of serenity in our worlds of calamity.

And yet…

This moment we know we should enjoy;

We can sense it in the crisp outpour of the stars.

Whatever moment we are in,

Wherever we are going,

We are everlasting in this one.

Author's Reflection

This poetry book has grown up with me.

Some poems I wrote on the purple carpeted floor of my room when I was 15 years old with tears streaking down my face, like *Infinite, Anyway* and *The Moths.*

As a grown woman, I embrace that clever, broken-hearted girl with so much tenderness. English, Language, and Chorus classes saved me and showed me there were ways to express what weighed on me.

Others came out of the soft ache of growing into my new skin during COVID lockdowns and job layoffs like *Gold Nothing*, *Hanahaki,* and *Acceptance.*

Some are direct quotes and memories from people I love the most, like *Bulldozer with a Smile* about being just like my dad, *Home* about the love I share with my siblings, and *Legacy* about my mom and incredibly strong female ancestors.

However, my favorite thing about poetry is that it can mean something different to each person, every time. I hope you find something that sticks with you.

With love,

Dana

Acknowledgments

To my Omar: I've said it before (in our wedding vows) but I'll say it again: it is no mistake that your name is an anagram for the Latin root for love, amor. You are magic incarnate.

To Aunt Denise: Your heart knows mine so well. I never would've started this without you. Thank you for listening and sharing your wisdom with me.

To my sister, Kaitlyn: My art is an extension of our bond and your belief in me. Thank you for always encouraging it... even late at night when you were trying to sleep in the bunkbed above mine. We are sisters in every life.

To my brother, Brendan: Turns out we really did get the superpowers that we said we did when we drank from my tea set or stepped on supermarket ads as kids. It just looks a little different. Your golden soul shines so bright. You inspire me in so many ways.

To Mom: You are the epitome of strength and softness wrapped into one. Thank you for making me believe in magic.

To Dad: My favorite part of writing poems as a kid (and an adult) was seeing your reaction to the really good ones. I know I'm your daughter, but I'm so proud of you.

To Becca and Lane: Both of you were so critical for me finding my voice in poetry. Bless you both for believing in my voice and encouraging me to keep going. I rediscovered my love of art because of both of you.

To so many of my close friends and family: I love you so much. I am so grateful for the whimsy and care you all inspire in me.

And last, but certainly not least, a million thank yous to my cousin, Michael, and Salty Books Publishing. To see a dream like writing this book come true means everything to me. Your kindness, encouragement, and voracity for life invigorated my writing spirit.

about the author

Dana Qadah grew up in small-town Armada, Michigan, where she first fell in love with poetry. She has a B.A. in Linguistics from Oakland University. She writes about eco-feminism, neurodivergence, and the nuance of being a human.

She lives with her sweetheart husband, Omar, and their two extremely spoiled cats, Mochi and Nacho, who kept her company into the wee hours of the night as she typed up all of these poems (previously handwritten) to create this amalgamation of words.

This is her first book, but certainly not her last mess.

www.ingramcontent.com/pod-product-compliance
Lightning Source LLC
Chambersburg PA
CBHW021343060726
47591CB00006B/2138

9781964354446